# The Music of Leaving

May. 2015 —

# The Music of Leaving

POEMS BY

## Tricia McCallum

**DEMETER**

DEMETER PRESS, BRADFORD, ONTARIO

Demeter Press
c/o Motherhood Initiative for Research and
 Community Involvement (MIRCI)
140 Holland St. West, P.O. 13022
Bradford, ON, L3Z 2Y5
Telephone: 905.775.9089
Email: info@demeterpress.org
Website: www.demeterpress.org

Demeter Press logo based on the sculpture, "Demeter" by
Maria-Luise Bodirsky <www.keramik-atelier.bodirsky.de>


Front cover artwork: Mayumi Terada, "curtain 010402." Courtesy:
James Hyman Gallery (London) and Robert Miller Gallery (New York).



Library and Archives Canada Cataloguing in Publication


McCallum, Tricia, 1952–, author
        The music of leaving : poems / by Tricia McCallum.

ISBN 978-1-927335-93-2 (pbk.)


Cataloguing data available from Library and Archives Canada.


Printed and Bound in Canada

MIX
Paper from
responsible sources
FSC® C004071

The Flower of Farewell

Somewhere the flower of farewell blooms and scatters
ceaselessly its pollen, which we breathe;
even in the winds that reach us first we breathe farewell.

—Rainer Maria Rilke, *Muzot mid October 1924*

# Contents

## III: Her Own Blues

# I.
# Everyone's Gone to the Moon

We look before and after
And pine for what is not:
Our sincerest laughter with some pain is fraught;
Our sweetest songs are those that tell
Of saddest thought.

—Percy Bysshe Shelley, *To a Skylark*

# Everyone's Gone to the Moon

*Why does it have to be your favourite song playing*
*Whenever you're the only one not asked to dance.*

There is a sadness in
the not being asked
that outdistances anything since.

When I showed up at the tea dance
I'd got it all wrong,
I thought they'd said
*dresses.*

You want it not to matter.
And it does,
so very much.

It's not that you even want
the boys
who don't want you.

You just want to feel
somehow
good enough.

Girls have it right nowadays.
They dance together.
They don't wait for a boy.
You can wait
a long time.

# Too Late Tomorrow

Fates ride on little moments.
Outcomes of entire lives can rest
on the seemingly miniscule.
Fresh from another of her parent's brawls
the little girl shuffles to school.
She needs a sign today
that the world is a safe place,
something better awaits.

This one afternoon in her life
could turn her around,
steer her through the minefields.
A comforting word,
a warm glance her way,
the right things happening
at just the right time.

You know this little girl.
Watch for her: the window is narrow.
But you are powerful.
She is waiting
for the smallest,
the sweetest of mercies
to be saved.

# Past Master

Among da Vinci's countless notebooks, all written in code,
or backwards, to ward off thieves,
is found a jotting that translates to:
"Tell me if I ever did a thing."
Hardest on himself,
his abandoned projects haunted him,
and those completed offer little solace:
scissors, the parachute, a clock with a minute hand, the helicopter,
the first contact lens.
An upstart, he sketched Mona Lisa, no doubt, just to keep us guessing.
Her lips *alone* took him 10 years.
Voracious curiosity fuelled him,
climbing a mountain outside of Milan to understand
*why the sky was blue.*
dissecting human cadavers to perfect his anatomical drawings and,
it is rumored, *lions!*
When he was commissioned to paint *The Last Supper*
he reluctantly put aside a joke book he was writing,
and throughout his life was convinced that if only we had wings
we could fly like birds.
*Imagine* this man's to-do lists:
"Have Avichenna's work on useful inventions translated."
"Buy mustard."
"Get a skull."

# While Visiting a School of Falconry in London

Large birds of prey are quite malodorous
close up like this,
bits of still-warm sinew and flesh wedged
deeply inside their fearsome hooked talons,
lodged within the recesses
of their dense coats.

The lesson is in progress.
Responding to the familiar whistle
the peregrine falcon appears suddenly
from the treetops,
looming, wings spread,
its grace incongruous
as it sweeps downward
by rote
toward accustomed rewards,

slowing the beat of its wings on approach,
the frenetic *wap wap, wap*, becoming the subdued
*whoo, whoo, whoo,*
its outsized yellow plasticine-like feet
coming to rest on the student's leather-clad arm
producing always the same look of sudden terror,
then simple astonishment,
as the raptor's full weight, its other-worldliness,
settles, completely,
onto its perch.

Their large, liquid, alien eyes,
their bobbing heads,
never still.
They hit our marks because it suits them.
The one in there
carried off a Yorkshire terrier
from the high street
once.
*Peregrinus,* meaning to wander.
They cannot,
they will not be
known.

# Subject Matters

Write poems you want to read,
counseled the famous poet.
And I do.
Not of the sunset
and whether it's pink
or more mauve than pink,
but of the gaunt young man
who watches it distractedly
from his boarding-house window
unsure
exactly
how to go on.

# Through the Porthole

I awake in the early light
to the smack of water between the hulls.
Something draws me to the tiny porthole by my berth,
not a sound really, more a sensation.
And there on the horizon
looms an ocean liner of such size
it appears mythic.

All glinting steel and glass,
a beacon under the new sun,
this monolith of turbines and chrome
cutting a swath a football field wide.

So far away
that neither the bellowing of her engines
nor the roar of her wake reach me,
rendering her eerily mirage-like,
a paint-by-number colossus,
frozen in a cement sea.

Too far away for me to decipher details
so I settle for only imagining
the early morning risers
now assembling on her decks,
settling into chairs with their first coffee,
breathing in the panorama before them.

Conversation would be hushed, expectant,
another idyllic day at sea ahead.

But do they see me?
my tiny sailboat moored off a small island,
might they conjure me as I do them,
whether I am awake yet,
where I sail to, from,
her name painted on the bow?

Will some raise their binoculars to learn more,
watching as I fade, inexorably,
into the shimmer of the new day?

# Are You From Around Here?

What a strange place this is
where people apologize
after accidentally touching
on the subway
and advertise for friends
in the Saturday paper.

What a sad place this is
where lives are expended over real estate
and happiness is one pill away.

A lonely place
where tiny children carry keys
to enter empty houses after school –
desperate, too
where speed dating allows for
only a rundown of business bios
before hearing "Next."

But miraculous, too
when amidst it all
the two of us
have managed to create
a few moments
of pure joy.

# Three Years

The little face stares out at me
from the faded poster
in the front window of the Tops Market,
partially obscured by
an ad for Downy,
and one for L'il Debbie's Snack Cakes:
*Buy one get one free.*

Stephen. His name is Stephen.
Quick math tells me
he's been missing three years.
Makes him nine now.
This would not quite
be his face anymore.

The poster is faded, curled at the edges.
It needs to be replaced, updated.
What are they waiting for.
Stephen looks straight ahead,
and will tomorrow, from the same place.
With the same face.
Passive, calm.
Time goes on.
He is waiting for us
to find him.

# Hallmark

Wrinkles form despite the miraculous claims.
A long red hair ends up in the semi-gloss.
The newest cereal promises vigour
like you've never known.
But I never really noticed a difference,
did you?

Sometimes don't you just get tired
Of saying "Onwards."
Sometimes building a life on top of all this pain
is too much work.
The greeting cards all start to look the same,
and standing in the drugstore you become annoyed
because you realize
you never actually saw a daisy
that looked like that.
A baby so composed,
A mother so happy.
A world so right.

# The Way to Go

I don't want to die
In an ambulance:
It's such a cliché.
Or in line at Ralph's,
where the people waiting behind will blame
the already-traumatized cashier for something
clearly my fault.

I don't want to die
alone in a hospital room
at four in the morning,
which I read that most of us do,
because it lacks romance and nuance
and just about everything else.

Nor in a convalescent home,
at the end of a quiet sterile hallway
two hours before anyone even notices
and not a spot of lipstick on,
all tucked in so I won't make a fuss.

I want to die
while arguing for pro-choice
with a bunch of rabid fundamentalists,
knowing I've been heard.

I want to die
on a Gold Wing motorcycle
heading south on Highway One,
Van Morrison on the headphones,
the vagabond road ahead
beckoning me by name.

Or this:
Put me in a sloop headed south
on a boisterous, wine-dark sea,
singing,
at the top of my lungs,
*Into the Mystic.*

# In What World

They say "bleeding heart"
like it's a bad thing.
There's judgment in it too,
as if being tolerant means
you don't quite comprehend all the facts.

They say don't acknowledge
the kid with the squeegee at the stoplight:
Fiddle with your radio instead.
Because once they lock eyes with you,
apparently it's already
too late.

# If This Is Your Final Destination, Welcome Home

Always the smell of tiger balm
takes me back to Kuala Lumpur in 1980,
the sweltering airstrips,
the sea of expectant upturned faces
of the refugees waiting en masse
at the bottom of the plane's stairs,
on their way to Canada
and to second lives.

Plane load after plane load,
week after week, four years running,
we ferried them across oceans.
After days and sometimes weeks in crowded busses
they waited to be next in line,
these survivors of Pol Pot and his merciless Khmer Rouge,
these survivors of unimaginable horror.
We delivered them to Montreal and to Toronto,
away from all they had known,
everything they owned in tidy bundles at their feet.

We chose our words carefully for the interpreter,
but how to prepare them for what lay ahead?
Where to begin.
How do you tell someone how cold feels?

We played them music we wanted them to hear,
hits of the day, Blondie, REO Speedwagon,
handed out sandwiches and Pampers and wet naps.
They in turn watched our every move,
accepted anything given to them, suspiciously at first,
then with vigorously nodding heads, pouring forth their thanks,
holding up their solemn, silent babies proudly for us to hold.
When the cabin lights dimmed,
hearing their guarded whispers to one another
sharing late night confessions in the dark above the ocean,
these people for whom nothing on earth
could be surprising.

Even when I urged them up the aircraft stairs,
beckoned them toward me,
they held back, tentative,
it was only when I descended the stairs,
took the first of them by the hand,
would they dare take the first step
toward this unimaginable freedom.

I see their faces clearly even now.
Who among us could possibly measure
the courage we asked of them.

# Eulogies

I live beside an abandoned cemetery,
and from my kitchen window on moonlit nights
I can see the gravestones perfectly,
sticking haphazardly out of the weeds
like stubby gray thumbs.

No roses are carefully placed there in remembrance,
no cars for Sunday visits.
Save for the odd, curious soul,
these are the forgotten.

In daylight
I clear the pock-marked stones of debris
to glean what I can,
committing what is written there to memory,
inventing stories for each.

At night
As I wash the plates and cups
I gaze at each grave in turn
utter their stories one by one
and whisper,
*I remember.*

# The Gift of Donovan

A frigid November day in Barrie, Ontario, 1967.
Wednesday, I remember.
We had just come from Novena Devotions.
Mark led me downtown to the town's one record store,
"For a surprise," he said.
The proprietor was in on this, I soon realized,
watching him head
to the stacks of wooden slots on the wall
and retrieve a 45 disc in its sturdy cardboard sleeve.

The needle on the vinyl began dispensing a melody
then Donovan's innocent accented voice wafted through the small shop,
*Colour sky havana lake*
*Colour sky rose carmethene*
*Alizarian crimson...*

The bewitching refrain,
*Lord, kiss me once more*
*Fill me with song*
*Allah, kiss me once more*
*That I may, that I may...*
*Wear my love like heaven...*
Worlds, colours I had not yet heard of,
at the age of 15, yet,
I sensed the magic of which he sang.

Dared to think these were places
I might go to.

I went on to my life, Mark to his.
Not long after he died, still a young man,
never giving me the chance to thank him
for his gifts that day,
for seeing me in a way I had never seen myself,
as a girl worthy of such lavish forethought
for giving me,
in that dead-end town,
an impossibly beautiful song.

# Perfectly Sad

The swing set across the road creaks and sways
this January morning.
It paints the perfect picture of sadness.
A textbook definition for anyone to see.
As if in collusion with the light and wind,
It sits there in stark detail against the bleak horizon,
snow collecting in its rusting joints.

The gargantuan uprooted tree by the river,
hanging on by its slim tortured roots,
It too knows.
The man alone in the coffee shop reading
yet not reading,
the woman at the bus stop in the cold
her broken shoes,
her cheap handbag hard against her heart
shaking her head,
*No, no. no.*

# Sisters

Almost objectively
I watched you both today
wading ahead of me
deeper into Wasaga's waters.

Two beautiful confident women
reveling in a shared remembrance,
your heads thrown back in easy laughter.

For the youngest sister
who followed behind
the moment crystallized
like stop action in film.

It brought with it
the simple realization
of how lucky we were
to have loved one another,
to have found friends in one another
along the way.

In years hence
when I consider our lives together,
it is this moment
on that brilliant July day
I will hold the most dear.

# Turn Left at the Lilies

Young James of Kerry,
do you know you have the face of Oscar Wilde,
and a sadness behind your eyes
even a stranger can see.

You seek solace among tombstones, it seems.
It's where I met you, that bitter windswept day,
roaming this ancient graveyard
that lies hard by the sea.

There's a set of resignation in your shoulders.
For one so young your pace is measured.
There is nowhere else you have to be.

When I ask for directions,
you tell me matter-of-factly,
in your lilting brogue,
"Down the road: turn left at the lilies,"
as if nothing could be simpler.

On a weekday morning in the rain
this is where you have come.
Where did your dreams go, James?
Why is this enough?

# Fraud

You think you're writing poetry
and then while waiting for the dentist,
you read one in *The New Yorker*
about elephants,
tied together, heads positioned down,
being paraded in a long line
through the Queens Midtown Tunnel after midnight,
on their way to a circus downtown,
blinders on to ward off car headlights,
forever away from their home
and the wild,
these creatures who hug using their trunks,
who have a membrane in their forehead
able to produce infrasound that connect their herds
across vast distances, even through vegetation,
these creatures who mourn their dead,
who will bend back the steel bars of their cages
in their fervor to reunite.

The dentist calls your name, you put down the magazine,
and you just want to stop writing
what you have,
for all these years,
fraudulently
been calling poetry.

# Glowing Tribute

There's this girl I know in Toronto
who goes to Buffalo to shop
for the bargains on Bill Blass sheets
and with her parents to Polish nights in Orillia
where she says she wouldn't be caught dead if the perogies
weren't to absolutely die.

She takes her vacations in Warsaw almost every year
because she tells me the deals on crystal are incredible
and she can stay cheap with her Aunt Stenya.

It's not like Mary isn't into Canada –
she did Banff in '82
and drove all by herself to Prince Edward Island in '84
where by the way she lucked in
to a fabulous villa timeshare in the Caymans
because thanks to God she had American Express on her.

In the back window of her Beamer with the Blaupunkt
there's one of those Canadian flag stickers and it glows at night
I mean what do you want from her
it isn't like she was born here.

# Come Back

My gums are bleeding again.
There's a stack of papers that need attention
But I can't find my glasses.
My truck is making that funny noise.

I sleep too late
Because no one wakes me.
I don't write
I feel it's all been said.

Your point's been made:
I am selfish and fickle,
Say whatever you like.
Come back.

# The Slide

The playground looks no different
now,
one year later.
Children play on the same swings,
studiously carve out roads in the sandbox,
hop aboard the hurtling roundabout,
squealing.

And over there, see them,
lining up to climb the stairs
of the giant metal slide
that sits, unaltered still,
atop its pad of
thick uneven concrete.

No question: it's a bad design.
Anyone can see that:
The guardrails are too shallow,
the descent too steep.
It would take but an instant
For things to go wrong,
A mother might not even see it.
Dipping into her purse for a lozenge.
It would be that quick.
Quick enough
for everything she had ever known,
held true,
to change.

# By the Wayside

On the Jersey Shore in Cape May there's a motel called
*By the Wayside.*
Out front there's a 20-foot statue of Peter Pan
which the owner built
because he said every time  he looked at it
he was reminded of happy endings.

Moira the motel lady, that's how I am known.
Lots of year-rounds as we call them,
tenants who call this home.
In Room 2B there's a tiny Japanese man from San Francisco
who has a compulsion to check envelopes before sealing them
to make sure his daughter isn't inside.
He lives in constant terror
that he will mail her away forever.

The gorgeous Josh one floor above bartends nights
at a restaurant down the shore
where he says he'd never be caught dead
under normal circumstances.
But nothing's been normal, he says, since
Manhattan's theatre world hung him out to dry.
Alice next to the office visits to have her makeup done on slow nights.
She left her husband of 30 years
the day she found his note to her on the kitchen table

signed with both his first
and last name.

The pain is in the details, the small things.
It's in the smell of baby aspirin
and in watching a mother stoop down to painstakingly
wipe her child's dirty face.
It's in a line of baby clothes hanging outside to dry.
In the sound of her name:
Amelia.
We were shoe shopping.
I was filling the parking meter and she stepped away
for an instant,
And I moved from that life to this,
my husband's anger still  loud in my head.
where summers are a blur and where
in winter
it is easy to disappear.

# II.
# Impossible Gardens

I didn't trust it for a moment
but I drank it anyway,
the wine of my own poetry.

It gave me the daring to take hold
of the darkness and tear it down
and cut it into little pieces.

—Lala, fourteenth century Persian poet,
"I didn't trust it for a moment" from *Naked Songs*

# Thirst

The sun was hotter:
You can tell.
Look at the people squinting against it in photos, then.
Everything washed out by glare:
Faces, thoughts, nuance,
all detail surrendered.
We could be anybody.

The backyards are parched.
Look at them.
It hurt to walk on the grass.
We lay in barren backyards
chain-smoking and eating fluorescent cheesies,
swilling scarlet soda.
We slathered butter on our chests.
Everyone was burned raw.
Everyone looked happy.

Nothing could go wrong.
Caution was ahead of us.
Men were above us,
landing on the moon.

# There's Always the Guy

There's always the guy
At pub closings
Mall food courts
Wedding dinners.

He wants to sit you down
Straighten you out.
Tell you how things work.
You have it all wrong, you see.
He laughs in your face.

You listen
Because it's late, or it's early,
You have nowhere to go
And no one waiting.

His oldest kid is 27, hasn't seen him in years,
but good riddance.
And three exes, somewhere.
*Hey, where do you think you're going?*
He's yelling at your back.
*Wait: Let me tell you about love.*

# Beautiful Dreamer

I could see her through the skinny glass panel
that ran down the side of the classroom door.
Following my after-school detention I had been drawn there
by the sounds of music,
incongruous in a place like this,
devoted so rigorously to the three R's.

Oblivious of her onlooker, I saw Sister Clara alongside her desk,
eyes closed,
swaying to the song *Beautiful Dreamer*
wafting from a record player on her desk.

*Beautiful Dreamer, Wake unto me* ...the singer crooned,
and as he sang she suddenly reached down,
lifted up the folds of her voluminous habit in both arms
and sashayed lightly up and down
between the rows of wooden desks,
her face a study in joy.

My mathematics teacher, a math genius, some said.
Stern, unforgiving, sad somehow.
But not here, not now.
The song over, she headed briskly for the door,
and even though my heart galloped in fright,
I did not move,
incapable of looking away.

# Too Cold for Snow

At this temperature
the wind sticks in your throat
like a stubborn lozenge.
Snow binds to everything like beach tar.
Even the dogs hang back in the morning,
extending timorous paws across the threshold
reluctantly.

Braving the trip into town
I hear Lightfoot singing "Rainy Day People" on Canoe FM,
pass three tow trucks and my neighbour
Henry on his snowmobile in a balaclava.
His wife, Sondra, is out of the woods, he shouts, pulling alongside,
but there is no joy in the telling.

No bear, moose, not even a deer to be seen this trip.
They ride this one out in caves and dens,
smarter than us.
In town Shirley at the Kozy Korner has my menu
on the table before I sit down,
launching into a diatribe on husband number three.
She's dyed her hair again, purple red this time. I lie,
tell her I like it.
What's one more lie to Shirley,
who's heard a lifetime of them?

The owner of the Dollar Store barrels in for a coffee to go,
complaining to no one in particular about his generator that's seized,
then Grace on her lunch from Foodland, who squeezes in beside me.
Her daughter moved to the city last year, hasn't been back,
and did I hear she's "born again."

We eat our fried egg sandwiches bundled up in scarves and toques,
the cold bone-deep,
so much energy spent just staying warm.
On the way home Donnie on the radio forecasts more of the same,
only colder.

# The Trouble with Science

If it's true
as grim neurologists now claim,
that our memory is far from intact,
that the very process by which we retrieve the past
is flawed, random, that it plays fast and loose with
fact, detail, even colour,
then how exactly do I recollect
precisely,
*us.*

If it's all up for grabs,
all bets off,
what was true?
The way you looked at me that evening
on the boardwalk,
was it as tender as I picture it now?
And your kiss. As deeply felt?
Did you profess your love in three languages
or was it just two?
Before you round the corner do you actually
turn to look at me
one last time?
Are you in the blue shirt
or the red?
Are those actual tears?

But science falls short. It overlooks
the power of the human heart
which has a memory all its own,
where the moments of our lives never alter,
fade
or grow old.
Where a look remains as tender
as when first it was delivered,
and a heart quickens just as it once did.
Yearning as fervent,
passion as acute.
And in that special place
the moments worth remembering
lie in wait for us, inviolate,
undefiled by time
or faulty synapse.

# Punch and Judy

Forget years, weeks,
minutes.
Narrow it down further.
The harried mother leaves the stroller unattended for two,
maybe three seconds,
a blip, not even,
in the massive rollout of time.

Count them down with me.
*One thousand* ... See how it's long enough
for a rollback of the pram down the subway stairs,
gathering momentum,
*two thousand,*
bouncing almost giddily now,
one of those pricey buggies
with the perfect suspension.

*Three thousand,*
Yes, now would be the perfect time
to produce a first responder at the bottom
gallantly returning the baby unharmed to the top
before rushing off to the trading floor.

When are subway stairs in New York City
ever empty,
you may well ask, dear reader.
How do any of us make it this far, I say,
when two seconds is all it takes for a mother
to be in need of a miracle
that never comes.
The right turn meant to be a left turn,
the unbalanced ladder that is scaled anyway,
the side rail on a children's slide
awaiting the simplest of repairs,
the lipstick
that needs freshening in the car's rear-view.

We can never take enough care.
*Four thousand.*
Scramble the hazmat suits.
Cue Punch and Judy.

# Why Worry

We sit on vast tectonic plates
equivalent in thickness
to the skin of an apple,
tread
on the filament of a spider's web.

Beneath,
a vast pool of molten rock,
magma so hot it burns
clear through the Earth's crust
up to the surface.

Volcanoes result.
Erupt. Decimate.
Settle back.

Did you hear me?
The skin of an apple
determines our fate.

# The Most Expectant Month

The air smells like mud in April.
There is no warmth to be had.
Everything yearns to break free
from the stubborn clutches of the forest floor.
But it's early yet.
April expects much,
but delivers
meagerly.

Tiny birds perch nervously on brittle branches,
more tentative than ever,
trilling, half-heartedly,
knowing no downy beds await them,
their nourishment still hard-won.

After a sudden string of warmer days
the lake water slowly escapes its sheath
and shimmers timidly in the scant light,
wary of this newfound freedom.

There, offshore,
the resident heron steps boldly from the slick rock
to test the waters
one elegant leg at a time.

# The Present

There are winds so ferocious
ancient nations have gone to war against them
in full battledress, knives raised.
Can we really know a world
where such magic happened before us,
or merely inhabit it.
Within our paltry space and time
we learn, stumble, stand erect again,
and are then gone,
an instant, no more, given us,
all that came before us
unknowable,
all to come after
a dream.

# The Care and Share

I'm due at the "Care and Share" thrift store
in this frozen outpost where I volunteer
twice a week,
where outsiders are viewed suspiciously,
and more people smoke than don't,
where politicians make speeches
about the permanently unemployed
and the permanently unemployed
make speeches about their exes,
the weather, and *The Young and the Restless.*

They carry the same slack-jawed look of disappointment
I've seen in small towns all my life,
as if they checked it off in a column somewhere.
It's in the way they speak to their children,
the way they distrust happiness,
push the hair out of their eyes,
open the door to leave,
the way they wave goodbye.

I keep a lookout for shoes for Helen, for her three kids under five,
Pete needs a suit, he's got a wedding in the city in June.
And Leonard. Shy sad Leonard wants a book on pirates.
Anything about pirates.

These single moms, these disaffected souls,
all the damaged trooping in like clockwork,
resignation their calling card,
looking for a find,
for deals and freebies,
something that will make a difference,
knowing nothing ever will.

# Empathy

Some people you only have to look at
to know they have not felt the agony you have.
Oh, maybe they lost someone once a long time ago
but you somehow know they've forgotten that pain,
exactly what it feels like,
they can't reach out and touch it anymore,
can't imagine yours.

The woman in her house with her new carpeting, her kids,
Jason's five now, *Where does the time go?*
and Howard, how he always plays golf on Saturdays but
*It gets him out of my hair.*

Life, the daily grind of it
seems easy for her
because Howard is home with the kids
in the backyard
waiting for her
to show off his new clubs.

# Enough

A barbecue and swim after work had brought us together
around the campfire that summer evening,
An impromptu thing teenagers do best:
*You bring the beer. I'll bring the chips.*

I watched her run up from the water laughing.
As I write this, her name comes back to me: Yvonne.
Fresh from her swim she stood close to the fire
in her yellow bikini
drying her waist-length blue-black hair with a towel.

She seemed so utterly assured of herself in the task at hand,
so composed for a young girl,
tossing her head languidly from side to side
then taking a large hounds tooth comb and slowly pulling it through
that hair of hers.

She must have known we all followed her every move,
couldn't help but know it by the silence
that had enveloped her ritual,
the flames casting an unreal glow
on that flawless form and face.

The men particularly stared in awe
at this goddess from Okinawa who'd ended up
in our backwater of all places,
in their midst.

I watched the men's faces watching her
that night,
knowing even at sixteen I would never possess the audacity
that was Miss Yvonne Tsubone's that night,
and for as long as it lasted,
that which comes from sheer and absolute physical beauty,
a calling card that says,
without words:
*I am perfect just as I am:*
*what I am is*
*enough.*

# Points for Trying

I was good to animals and small children.
Made room for the guy on the streetcar
who talked to himself.
Even gave him a few bucks.
But truth be told:
I never invited him home to tea.

Didn't always take the easiest way,
but certainly enough times.
And, yes, vanity got in the way,
more than once –
the fight back from an ugly girlhood.

I frittered away talent,
pearls to swine, some might say,
churning out *Fortune 500* articles for rent money,
giving my all on corporate press tours,
with no energy left for the poem.
*But a girl's got to make a living,*
long seemed a worthy excuse.

The world gives you too many reasons
to feel you're not quite
good enough, talented enough.
Accomplished enough.
And there was I –
Listening intently
to each
and every one.

# The Island Dog

He is everyone's,
yet he is no one's.
Vacationers arrive, discover him,
dote on him for two weeks,
then disappear.

He is their holiday project.
A story they'll tell over dinner at home.
Some allow him in, to sleep at the foot of their beds,
to guard their front door.
Some even toy with the idea of a rescue,
Could we, should we? Shots? Papers?
Questions asked,
with the exuberance of the relaxed and the happy,
but as the time to leave draws near,
Reality encroaches, the idea stalls.

A new band takes their place,
The island dog waits,
Knowing it will take only one,
One, to give him a name that won't change,
One, to call it out in the dark
should he wander too far.
One, to call to him
and him alone:
*Come home.*

# The Sleepover

A Friday morning, Grade Six, and all anyone
could hear was the conspiratorial talk
of the girls' sleepover
planned for that night.
I kept waiting for the tap on my shoulder
and the invite whispered
in my ear. Stayed close to the girl's cabal
at recesses and long after school until it finally
sunk in. My face in the pillow that night, the fear
I would drown in my tears.
There were a thousand little deaths,
strung out until morning.
How can such moments not define us?
Not ruin us
for anything good
that might ever come after.

# Words Enough

What this poet wants is simple, really.
To write something that would hold
you in thrall
from the first word.
You'd be powerless before my visions,
stunned how I present this world
where you live:
A world you thought you knew.

I'd show you the sad light of a chill February morning,
and in it a little boy walking,
unwashed, head down,
to school.
The look on a young girl's face when
at the last minute
another is chosen.
Inside my poem you'd watch a mother,
helpless before her child's pain.

You'd see things for the first time in my poem,
wonder what you've been doing
all this time.

This poem would make sense of it all.
There is nothing it could not do.
You'd come to this poem for answers
and you would find them all
there.

# Of Distant Shores

The sense of smell
is the one most closely linked
with memory,
proven again yesterday when I brushed past
a stand of lavender and was instantly flung back
to the Grade Five classroom,
the glamorous, fragrant
Miss Beauchesne in full sail,
reading to us from *Treasure Island* one bleak winter morning,
filling our heads with inconceivable
stories of immense seas and the sailors upon them
and tropics where the cold couldn't reach
on shores so distant, scarcely imaginable
to those of us listening keenly,
seated at our rigid wooden desks set
in perfectly straight lines
within our small Ontario schoolhouse,
bounded by the thick February ice,
her magnificent purply scent wafting
up and down the aisles with her
as she walked each one,
languidly,
in turn,
and delivered to us the world.

# What Remains

On a tiny Bahamian island,
we assemble for a reading,
this crowd of rovers and ex-pats and sailors.
My turn: I share a poem I wrote about my mother,
her sudden profound loss.
The riches she left me.

After, at the sea's edge,
an elderly gentleman approached me, cautiously,
thoughtfully.
"Will someone write poems like that about you
after you die?" he asked,
and seemed genuinely curious about my answer.

Of course he was asking about himself.
Such things are always about ourselves.
I laughed and said I didn't know.
But I did.
I knew.

# At Rest

He can be found at the cemetery most afternoons
for as long as he can stand the heat, or the cold.
By the hour he sits there in sight of her grave
on a small iron bench.
It is inscribed in memory of another,
yet it seems meant just for him.

On the rare days we share the bench
I am always the first to grow restless,
to suggest home.
For me it is an ominous place,
unkind.

*I talk to her,* he says warily,
searching my face for signs of judgment,
worry.
Talk away, I tell him.
Take comfort where you can.

Together they had forged a life
in a country not their own,
bathed their babies, taken joy.
She was the only one who knew him
when he was young.

# Passing Sounds

Even the graveyards speak
in Ireland,
but 'tis no surprise, after all,
in this anachronistic land
where storytellers are cherished
and still abound,
and cannot be silenced by
mere death.

The faces of the worn stones call out
one by one,
the granite chipped out letter by letter with
bits of verse, meditations to ponder,
songs for the singing.
A lifetime is not nearly enough
for the stories they need tell.
Listen to the dead.

# One Favour

In all those years,
one thing she asked of him,
to sit up with her the long night through
as she waited word of her mother,
sick, suddenly, and so very far away.

The call came in the small secret hours of morning
and she crept to the phone
to hear the worst she could imagine,
her mother gone from her,
forever,
in a place she would never know,
worlds away.

Nursing tea she watched daylight
fill the window.
By the time he emerged from the bedroom
to stand before her,
she had accepted
yet another ending.

# Washed Up

When did everyone start washing with Purell
every time you look around?
As if we could prevent anything,
stop germs
if they have any interest in us
whatsoever.

When did greeting cards start costing 12 dollars.
For real.
No one else complains:
The guy in front of me buys four.
Unfazed.

And while I'm at it
when did it become a crime
to dress.
*You're so dressed up,*
spat out
like the worst possible indictment.
And the unforgivable,
me, in heels and
ok, maybe
a sequined brooch.

# This Instead

There's a hole in the sprinkler
and the patio needs sweeping
but not now.
Let's use summer for something else,
do what people used to do
in sunshine.
Lie together on old blankets
beside a river we happen upon.
Stare up at the blue holding hands,
blurting out whatever comes to us.
Time will have no sway.
We'll just lie there
for hours.
Let the day take us
until we are counting
the stars.

# Know You Were Here

Tease out the meaning of things.
Have all of this count
For something.
Make it your life's work.

Look up from your book, your ledger,
Your slumber.
Messages are waiting.
The sun sets down at the dock in five minutes.
Someone has something to show you,
Drop everything.

We are granted a finite amount
of absolutely
everything.
Listen for the unspoken.
Pop your collar.
Shoot your cuffs.
Know you were here.

# III.
# Her Own Blues

Why We Are Truly a Nation

Because we rage inside
the old boundaries,
like a young girl leaving the Church,
scared of her parents.

Because we all dream of saving
the shaggy, dung-caked buffalo,
shielding the herd with our bodies.

Because grief unites us,
like the locked antlers of moose
who die on their knees in pairs.

—William Matthews

# Reverence

I can't step into a church without being reminded of Leo.
I see him, leaning heavily on his cane, waiting in the vestibule
to usher the parishioners to their seats,
his labored gait up the aisle, one leg stiff,
the shoulder of his Canadian Legion jacket
heavy with medals and ribbons.
The rubber tip of his cane
squeaks loudly against the polished floor.

The star resident at her mother's boarding-house,
my friend Linda said we should visit him.
He'd insisted,
and there had been toffees promised.
Restless and bored one spring day I relented,
followed Linda home and climbed the stairs lazily to Leo's room.
Unlike the others his door was open.
There was Leo, lying on his bed, his cane alongside,
rest the only respite from his affliction.

*Come in, close the door.*
*Feed my bird Charlie.*
I worried then about telling my mother this.
But Leo wasn't a stranger.
Everyone knew Leo.
Father Blackwell told us in catechism class
it was men like Leo who had kept us free.
The shabby room smelled of wet wool

from clothes drying on the radiator
and of Old Sail, his pipe tobacco.
A bowl of sweets beckoned by the bed.
Charlie was hopping about in his cage.

*Sit beside Leo, honey.*
A good Catholic girl, I did as the hero said.
The bristles of his beard stung my face,
his breath turned to a rasp.
I smelled something fetid on his breath.
When at last he released me,
Charlie was singing,
still.

# Jackknife

Up the rungs of the diving ladder one more time,
gripping the cold, unforgiving steel
with my shriveled bare toes, nine steps to the top,
reaching, it seemed,
to the sky.

Still in his work clothes, my father stands watching
from behind the chain-link fence surrounding the pool.
I knew he was coming,
I'd practiced all day for this.

I tiptoe along the pebbly surface
of the board and stand shivering at the very edge,
sneak a quick glance at the water so far below
speckled eerily now with fluorescent lights,
preparing to make this one count.

It's time.
Great lungfuls of air taken in,
the familiar flutter in my chest
as I bend my knees deeply, leaping upward
high as I can go,
then even higher, the board shuddering behind me,
trying to remember all his pointers at once:

*Don't look at the water: it's not going anywhere,*
dividing myself neatly in half, toes touched lightly to fingers,

the uncanny feeling of suspension in mid-air,
forcing my body straight again:
*Ramrod straight, now,*
*You're an arrow shot at the water,* then
down so fast, the world thundering past my ears,
slicing the surface crisply,
sculling quickly up,
the entire time thinking
of all that I did wrong.

On the way home I sit in gloom beside him,
close to tears, too tired to resist.
*You never see my best ones,*
I say out loud without thinking.
He pulls the car over, stares at my face,
hot now with embarrassment, and reaches for the towel
to rub my long hair dry.

*Lassie,* he says gently,
cupping my chin in his hand.
*To me, they are all your best ones.*

# Rewrites

I would have done it all differently.
Had you even hinted
this was our final scenario
I would have risen to the occasion,
played it out properly.

I would have looked my most beautiful,
uttering grand, dramatic soliloquies
on our time together
and life in general.
Your most casual comments
I would have catalogued
to listen to later.
I'd have studied you
while your weren't looking
taking mental notes
of each beautiful detail.

Your grabbing for my hand
as we walked
would have meant more to me
that night
than just something
you had a habit of doing.

I'd have prolonged our parting,
our usual kiss at the door,

kept your arms around me a second longer
and watched the back of you,
leaving.

Instead,
I dismissed you
almost casually,
as complacent lovers often do,
knowing there will be
a next time.

# Parallax

My memory has been good to you since you left.
It's taken you and buffed your sharp edges,
polished up your one-liners,
edited your conversations for wit
and sensitivity.

It's rationalized your selfishness and rather quick temper,
forgotten how you hated sharing a single bed,
inconvenience in general.
It even injects feeling into your empty phrases.
You'd love my memory of you.

I wouldn't advise you to come back.
You could never compete with it.
Even your eyes aren't that blue.

# Cathy Was Her Name

Imagine it's your mother lying there
on a stretcher in the hospital corridor,
awaiting a proper hospital bed and privacy.
Count the number of people streaming by.
Some noticing her fleetingly,
others, even worse, not at all.
In her drugged sleep she is unaware
that her gown has slipped from her frail shoulders
and that her mouth gapes open.
Should you speak directly to her she may awaken
long enough to cast you
a trembling, suspicious glance.

Now imagine this woman before,
in the days when people stopped her on a Glasgow street
to admire her red hair.
*Cathy,* you'd have called out to her, then.
And she'd have lit up in response.
God, she brought three young children to this country
by herself,
made a life for them.

Understand me: this woman lying here,
inert and powerless,
the one who sleeps her last days away
in a hospital hallway –
This was once a lassie to be reckoned with.

# None of Her Own

I am the woman
who cares for other people's children,
nipping at the corners
of the things real mothers do.

My decisions are temporary,
makeshift things,
my power borrowed.
*Let's see what your mother says,* is my refrain.
To parents I concede:
*But of course I'm not a mother...*

While they are mine
I fill their days with crafts, hikes, stories,
feverishly packing the visit with memories to last until the next,
lavishing on them attention they rarely get elsewhere.
*No hitting. No name-calling:* they know my rules well.

And when it comes time
I ship them back all scrubbed and exhausted
to their real lives,
shouting after them:
*Come back soon.*
*Miss you already,*

I watch them
run to their mothers
and once inside their arms
they do not even think
of looking back.

# Catch Up

Everybody loves a train at a distance –
Explains you and me perfectly.
The champion of the dine and dash,
calling for the cheque too soon.
Methodically, diabolically, keeping me
off balance.
Plans coming from you were vague,
up for sudden,
inexplicable change.
There was always someone on hold,
or in your lobby, waiting,
drumming her fingers.
Even when alone
we were never
quite
alone.
Off kilter, off guard,
I grew expert in the art of rationalization,
the game of catch-up.
It seemed you were always rounding a corner
in the distance
the moment I caught sight of you,
the belt of your flawlessly-tailored trench coat
flapping behind you
as you ran.

# Castoffs

I didn't say half of what I wanted
that day we met for the last time,
complaining about the weather
and working too hard,
giving you countless opening for reassuring words
which never came.

You didn't say half of what you should.
Not noticing I had cut my hair.
(Remember the time you begged me not to?)
Instead you seemed concerned with the lousy service
and asked about that blue shirt of yours.
Could I please try and find it, you said.
It was one your favorites.

I said things I never meant to,
that my life was better now,
less complicated,
wanting you to shake me,
tell me I was lying.

But you had plans, you said,
and worried about getting a cab
away from there,
and me.

By the way, I found your blue shirt.
I even put it on now and again.
It was one of your favorites.

# How I Lose You

It's not in anything said.
Not in the tilt of your head
or a particular tone of voice.
It's in the almost imperceptible –
The way you get into bed at night,
carefully.
The way you ask if I want anything,
politely.
You've stopped reprimanding me
for biting my nails,
stopped asking who was on the telephone.

Silences are suddenly uncomfortable.
The ease is gone,
as you will be,
soon.
The moment someone leaves you
they have left you long before.

# Following Seas

Remember –
How the sunlight hit the mainsail just so.
The water sloshed good-naturedly between the hulls.
Van Morrison crooned his latest
while the kettle sang on the tiny beat-up stove.
An old man on shore stood waving to us
for the longest time.

Remember
the fish we saw through our masks.
They looked like the drawings of a child
who'd just discovered colour.

Spent, slick with salt water,
we splurged on hot showers
and sang to one another across the deck.
Later
we lay at the bow for hours, wondering
how could a night possibly hold
so many stars.

# Kiss the Sweetness

The trouble is: we want more and more
and then more of this.

Only this morning: relaxing over coffee,
James Taylor singing "Fire and Rain,"
A tiny black and orange bird at the feeder
we'd never seen before,
the summer light just so
on the bed of daisies out front.
This very morning.

The word I am looking for is *savour.*
*Savour* this:
It will not –
oh, it cannot,
last.

# Legacy

The afternoon is fading.
Your naps are longer than ever,
the times you are alert
grow more precious.
Your lips move erratically
in sleep.
Before you wake this time
I memorize your face,
bathed in summer light,
aristocratic still.

I wish I could give you
your due, mother,
carve the language in tribute
just so,
detail the riches you leave me,
give your life back to you
in radiant verse.

*Oh, to be a poet*
I say lightly when she stirs.
*I'd write you something lovely.*
As I prop her pillows and smooth her hair
she stares into my face.
*You are my poem,* she says softly
and I laugh, dismissing it.

*You are my poem,*
she says again,
pausing between each word.

# One of These Gray Days

One of these gray days
I'll find a tear on my cheek
yet not remember shedding it
I'll marvel at how naive I was
how aware I've become
I'll dabble in the stock market
and own matching china.

I'll worry that my lover
is spending too much time
with his wife
I'll wait for movies to come on TV
books to come out in paperback
I'll find time for bridge.

One of these gray days
I'll feel silly in bare feet
never go without makeup
and pass on dessert
I'll buy clothes with important labels
at important little shops
where they'll call me by name
I'll no longer want children.

I'll begin to acquire a taste for martinis
which I'll serve at intimate gatherings

I'll worry about laugh lines
and know of a good surgeon.

I'll insist on ten hours sleep a night
and begin to dislike chocolate
I won't own jeans
I'll see several men casually
who'll know when not to call
what subjects not to mention
I'll invest wisely.

I won't find pratfalls funny anymore
just dangerous.
I'll think fiction is a waste of time
and worry about the wax from burning candles.

One of these gray days
I'll find a tear on my cheek
I don't remember shedding.

# Be Quiet: You're Talking

Tell me something I don't know.
That there are insects that can fly through the rain
without getting wet,
that wild optimism usually masks deep despair,
and Esther Williams hated the water.

That astronauts have the highest divorce rate,
redheads need more anaesthetic than others,
left-handed people die younger,
tears of grief have a chemical composition different
from all others,
Emily Dickinson didn't leave her room for twelve years,
and that Chinese doctors examine a patient's tongue first.

Enlighten me.
Fill me with awe.
Share ideas incandescent –
Or stop talking.

# Pentimento

Strange how the house looks smaller now,
stripped of furniture and pictures.
In every room demarcation lines on the walls and rugs
sketch out a faint pattern of where beds and tables sat.
The *For Sale* sign sits squarely on the front lawn,
almost dwarfing the tiny house behind.
Prospective buyers troop through,
asking cunning questions, jotting down square footage.
Yes, the attic is insulated. No,
no dishwasher. Is the furnace oil?

Questions are answered, bids made,
the house goes to the highest,
yet they know little of what is now theirs,
not of the six of us who called this place home
through 30 years,
the countless others who found shelter here,
of the laughter that ricocheted through these rooms,
the thousands of early morning gatherings over tea,
the late night revelries.

A girl once stood on the front steps
and tilted her face up
for her first kiss.
In the upstairs bedroom
a young man dressed for his wedding.

Brand new grandchildren crossed the threshold
in their mothers' arms.
Not long ago in a room off the hall
a husband watched his wife grow weaker,
powerless to stop it.

Only vestiges of us remain –
a lone Christmas bulb in the cubbyhole,
a ring of worn grass in the back where a birdbath sat,
the smell of Chantilly in a closet,
a stand of fading peonies that will bloom
the most vivid scarlet come summer.

If they look closely they may find something else;
a series of blurred marks on the kitchen door jamb,
the running tally of growing children,
then their children,
lines crowded together alongside dates and names
that no matter how hard they scrub
may refuse to disappear.

# Remember Us

*How have you been*
is what I say to my sister,
long estranged,
when what I mean is,
Who are you now
Are you still in there,
Do you remember us?

The summer days of pyjamas and chocolate,
in mom's cold basement in front of the TV,
game shows and reruns of *Get Smart,*
talking without talking,
a look said it all.
Nights at the drive-in movies,
laughing at the nervous boys,
the race from work up to the beach in borrowed cars,
towels thrown down, radio on, smokes at our side.
We *worked* on our tans,
that's the word we used,
planting ourselves there until the last possible minute,
the race home, laughing,
clocking in at work with seconds to spare,
quick kisses before parting.

Do you remember,
that last good summer?

# For Keeps

Why did I not grab every moment
and make it sing.
Look into people's faces and find stories there
to take me into my old age.

We don't take the time,
do we.
Blithely we pass untraveled roads,
agonizing instead about the minutiae of our lives,
pairs and doubles,
the matched sets of things.

What will we leave.
Fragments of ourselves
not the real thing.
The thing underneath it all
that makes our hearts beat,
gives breath to our dearest selves.

That –
That which is
the best of us,
somehow gets muddled,
then irrevocably lost,
in our blind rush toward
the rest.

Why did I not grab every moment
And make it sing.